This activity book belongs to:

There are lots of women who have achieved extraordinary things by following their hearts, talents and dreams. Adventure with just a few of these fantastically great women and see how you could change the world!

VOTES FOR WOMEN

Write your own story with Jane Austen

Jane Austen wrote in secret because in **1811** people did not think that women should have jobs. Nowadays, Jane's books are recognised as some of the best stories ever created.

Catherine Morland
Northanger Abbey

Elizabeth Bennet
Pride and Prejudice

If you were an author, what would you write about?

Mr Darcy
Pride and Prejudice

A story always has a great hero. Who is the hero in your story?

You can include their name, what they look like and what makes them great.

Emma Woodhouse
Emma

Mrs Norris
Mansfield Park

The hero usually has to overcome a villain or an enemy. Who will they be in your story?

You can include their name, what they look like and what makes them so terrible.

Sir Walter Elliot
Persuasion

A good story always has a great opening line.
Can you finish off this story?

It was a dark and stormy night.

_____

_____

_____

_____

_____

_____

_____

_____

HELP GERTRUDE EDERLE SWIM THE CHANNEL

In **1926** Gertrude Ederle became a world record breaker when she became the first woman to swim the English Channel.

ENGLAND

KINGSDOWN BEACH

★ FINISH

★ START

CAP GRIZ-NEZ

FRANCE

Which path should she take to cross the freezing cold English Channel?

Dot-to-dot fossil hunting with
Mary Anning

Until **1800** most people believed the earth was only thousands of years old. Then Mary Anning came along. She was an amazing fossil-hunter, and the fossils she found proved that the earth was actually millions of years old!

Join the dots to find fossils hidden in the sand.

PLESIOSAUR

PTEROSAUR

ICHTHYOSAUR

Mary found the skeletons of three amazing dinosaurs – Ichthyosaur, Plesiosaur and Pterosaur.

Crack the secret code with
Agent Fifi

Agent Fifi worked as a special agent during the Second World War. Fifi pretended to be a journalist, but she was really testing new spies to make sure they wouldn't give any important information away.

Can you crack the secret code? Use the code alphabet below to uncover the hidden messages.

A B C D E F G H I

J K L M N O P Q R

S T U V W X Y Z

SPOT THE DIFFERENCE WITH

MARY SEACOLE

Spot the difference between the two pictures. There are 10 to find.

In **1854** Mary Seacole travelled all the way from Jamaica to the Crimea to build a hospital to help injured soldiers from all the countries who were fighting in the Crimean War.

COLOUR IN THESE
FANTASTICALLY
GREAT
WOMEN

Anne Frank

SACAGAWEA

Rosa Parks

COCO
CHANEL

HOW WILL YOU

MARY
SEACOLE

GERTRUDE
EDERLE

Jane Austen

AMELIA EARHART

Agent Fifi

Mary Anning

change the WORLD?

Frida Kahlo

Marie Curie

EMMELINE PANKHURST

START ➤

Can you help them find their way out of the maze?

Find your way across the USA with SACAGAWEA

In **1804** Native American teenage girl, Sacagawea, helped a group of 40 male explorers, called the Corps of Discovery, find their way to the west of the USA. And she did the whole thing with a newborn baby on her back! They travelled 6400 kilometres through the Rocky Mountains, down rushing river rapids and through raging storms.

FINISH

COCO CHANEL

When fashion designer, Gabrielle Chanel or 'Coco', opened her first shop in Paris in **1910** she changed the way women dressed forever.

What would you design?

Colour your own swimming costume.

In **1918** Coco Chanel launched the first range of pyjamas for women. Before this, they were only worn by men!

Colour your own little black dress.

Colour your own pyjamas

Draw yourself differently with ...
Frida Kahlo

Mexican artist, Frida Kahlo used art to say exactly what she thought and felt – something unusual for women at the time!

Frida painted lots of self-portraits. Draw your own self-portrait in this frame. You can make it as different as you like!

Frida liked to paint animals, too. She used them to show what she was feeling. Frida painted dogs when she was making big decisions and she painted monkeys to show the importance of family.

What animal describes how you feel? Draw it in this frame.

ADVENTURE WITH AMELIA EARHART

In **1932** adventure-loving American pilot Amelia Earhart became the first woman ever to fly solo across the Atlantic Ocean. The journey took her 14 hours and 56 minutes!

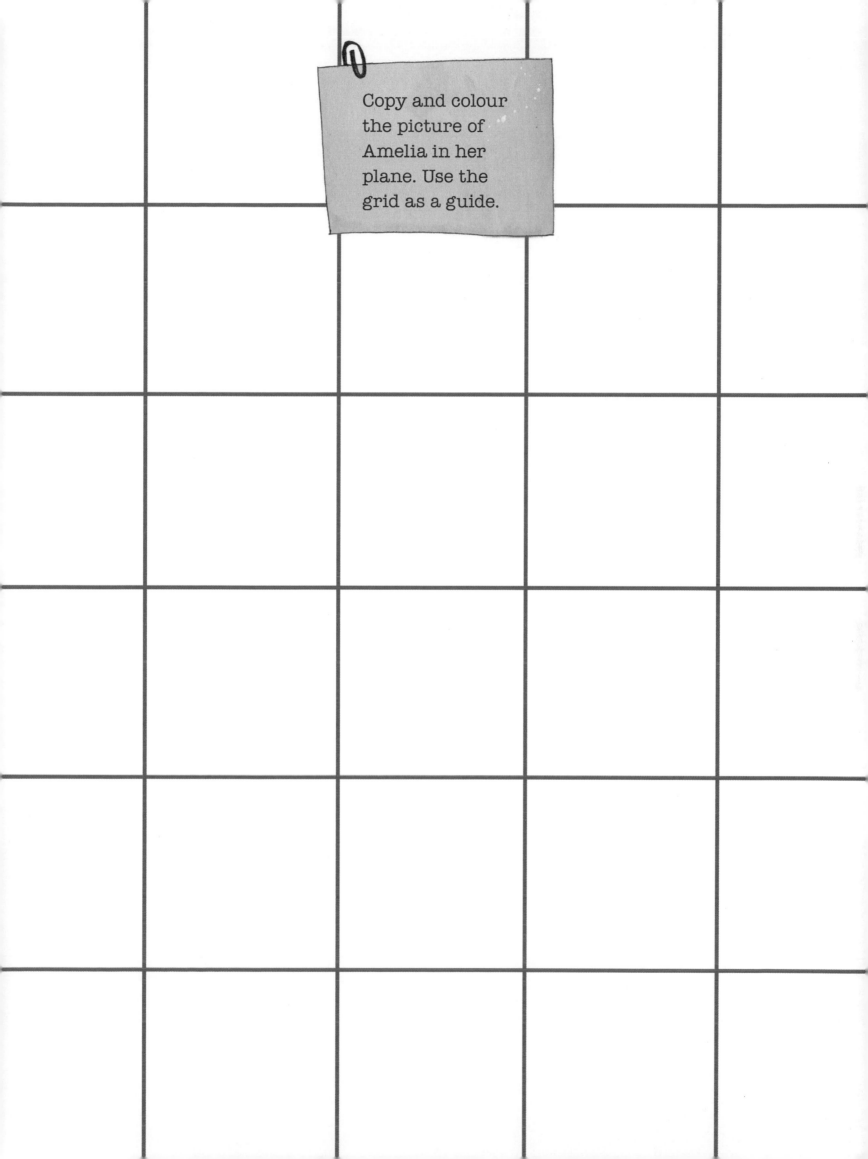

Copy and colour
the picture of
Amelia in her
plane. Use the
grid as a guide.

Keep a diary with

Anne Frank

During World War Two a thirteen-year-old Jewish girl called Anne Frank hid in a secret annexe with her family to avoid persecution. Anne kept a diary while she was in hiding. Today her diary is read by people all over the world.

Use the space below to write your own diary entry.

Anne stuck photographs of her family, friends and favourite things on the wall of her bedroom in the annexe.

Stick photographs or draw pictures of you and your family on this page.

MAKE THE NEWS WITH
{EMMELINE PANKHURST}

Emmeline Pankhurst and the suffragettes made the newspapers in **1903** when they used 'deeds not words' to campaign for women's right to vote. They interrupted political speeches, marched with banners and some protesters even chained themselves to the railings of important buildings. In **1918**, the law was finally changed – women aged over 30 were allowed to vote!

Write a news story on the opposite page about something you believe is really important. Decorate it with stickers.

You can use the words in the box below to help you.

Passionate	Protest	Law
Fair	Changed	Trouble
Determined	Inspire	People
Strong	Campaign	Believe

Headline

Write your story here

_____

_____

_____

_____

_____

_____

_____

_____

Draw a picture here

_____

_____

_____

Experiment with Marie Curie

Marie Curie was a brilliant scientist who studied radioactivity. While studying x-rays she discovered Radium, which can be used to treat people with cancer. Mary is the only woman to have won the Nobel Prize for Science *twice*!

What would an x-ray of your hand look like? Draw around your hand. You can add the bones in too, using this picture as a guide.

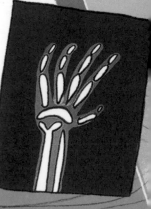

Protest inequality with **Rosa Parks**

Rosa Parks inspired a revolution in **1955** when she refused to give up her seat on the bus for a white passenger.

Design a poster with the words 'Stand up for what you believe'.

FANTASTICALLY
GREAT
WOMEN
POSTCARDS

Cut out the postcards on the
following pages and send them
to all the fantastically great
women in your life. Tell them
why you think they are
so amazing!

COCO CHANEL

MARY SEACOLE

SACAGAWEA

Jane Austen

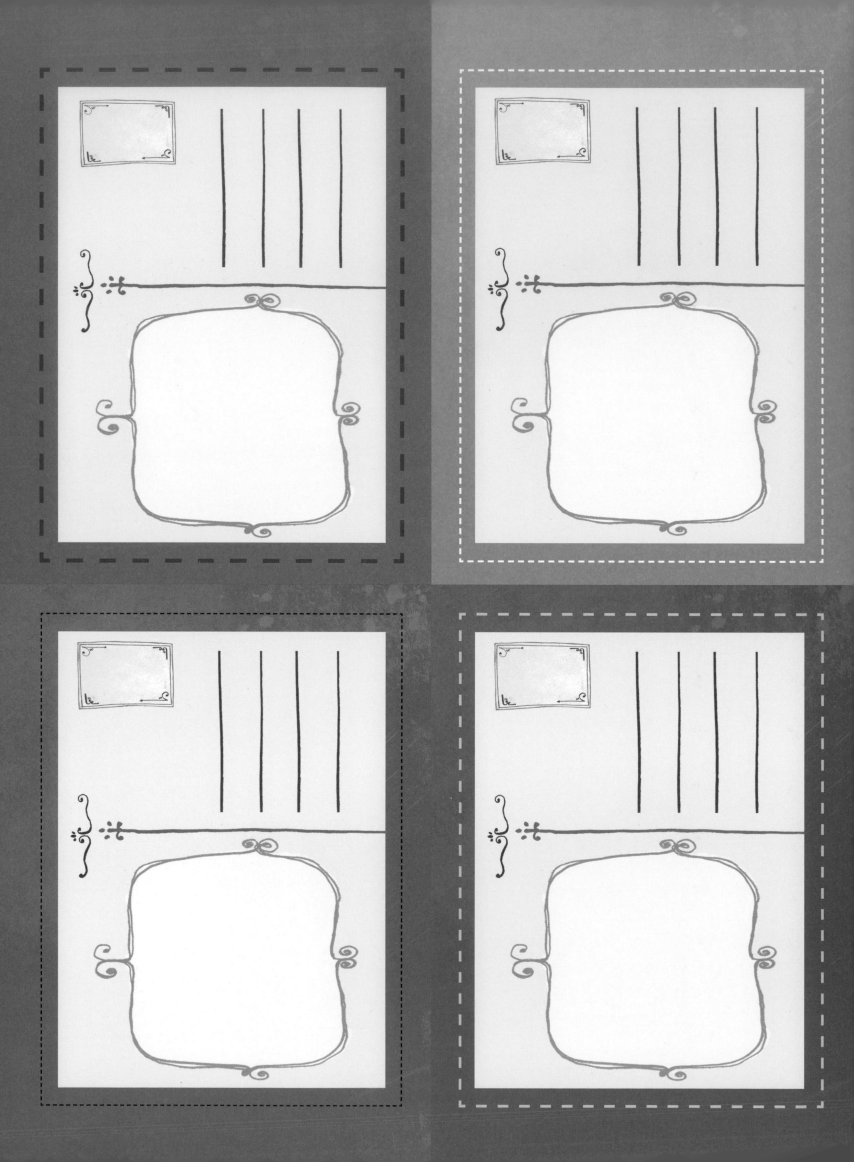

Rosa Parks

Anne Frank

Marie Curie

Frida Kahlo

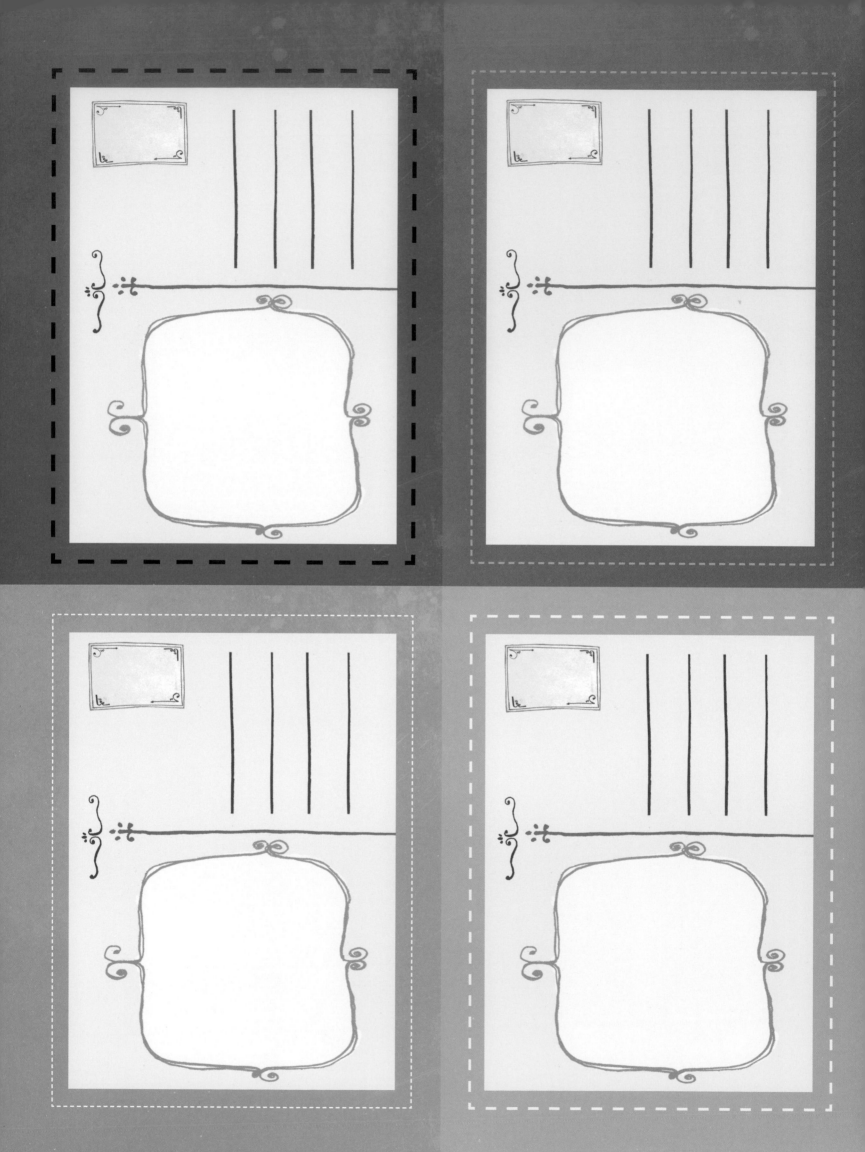

My Fantastically GREAT are... WOMEN

Draw the people you admire in this frame.

HOW ARE YOU GOING TO CHANGE THE WORLD?

The fantastically great women
in this book never gave up.

Write your own hopes and dreams on this page.

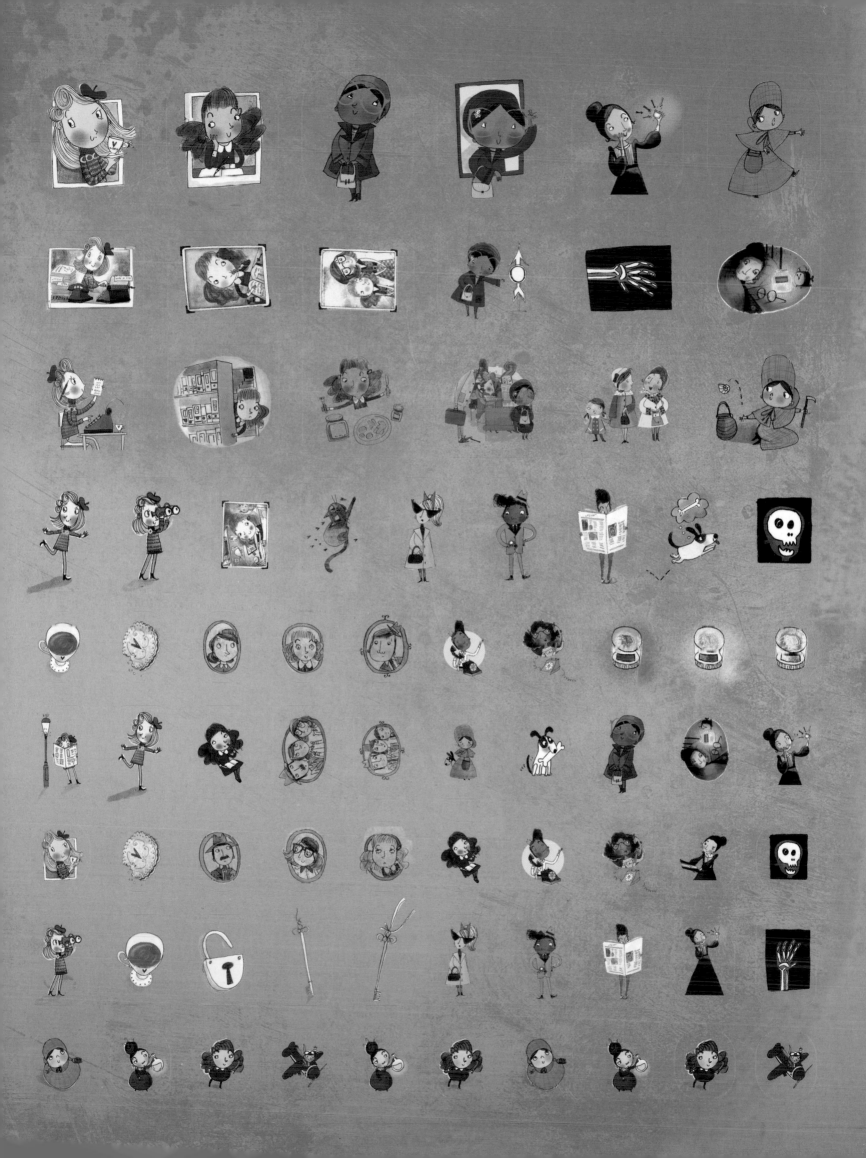